W9-BYZ-299

GREECE
the land
Sierra Adare

A Bobbie Kalman Book

The Lands, Peoples, and Cultures Series

Crabtree Publishing Company

The Lands, Peoples, and Cultures Series

Created by Bobbie Kalman

Editors
Virginia Mainprize
Greg Nickles
Ellen Rodger

Computer technology advisor
Robert MacGregor

Project development, writing, and design
Water Buffalo Books
Mark Sachner
Sabine Beaupré
MaryLee Knowlton

Separations and film
Dot 'n Line Image Inc.

Printer
Worzalla Publishing Company

Illustrations
Susan Tolonen: pages 10–11, back cover
Jim Chernishenko: map page 5

Special thanks to
The Greek Tourism Office and Office of the
Minister of Business, New York; Gonda
Van Steen, Department of Classics,
University of Arizona; the Panos family;
Marsha Baddeley

Photographs
Susan Alworth: page 23 (top); Archive/Photo Researchers: page 16; Frederick
Ayer/Photo Researchers: page 7; Corbis-Bettmann: page 17 (bottom); Marc
Crabtree: pages 1, 4, 31; Robert Fried/Tom Stack: page 18 (top); Margot
Granitsas/Photo Researchers: pages 20, 24 (top); Jalain/Explorer/Photo
Researchers: page 26 (top); Wolfgang Kaehler: pages 3, 10, 12, 13, 18 (bottom
left, bottom right), 19, 21 (bottom), 23 (bottom), 26 (bottom), 27, 28, 29, 30
(bottom); Noboru Komine/Photo Researchers: cover, page 21 (top); Francois
Le Diascorn/Photo Researchers: page 6; Loirat/Explorer/Photo Researchers:
page 8; Will & Deni McIntrye/Photo Researchers: pages 17 (top), 22;
Porterfield/Chickering/Photo Researchers: page 24 (bottom); Carl Purcell:
page 15; Tom Stack & Associates: page 9; Thouvenin/Explorer/Photo
Researchers: page 25; Vanni/Art Resource, NY: page 14;
Wysocki/Explorer/Photo Researchers: page 30 (top).

Front cover: Delphi was one of the most important religious centers of
ancient Greece. People went there from all over Greece and even from other
countries to worship the god Apollo.

Title page: The rocky landscape of this town in the Greek isles shows that the
islands are actually submerged mountain ranges whose tops jut above the
water's surface.

Back cover: Olives and olive oil have been a part of the Greek diet since
ancient times. This vase, which was made in the sixth century BC, shows
men harvesting ripe olives by beating an olive tree with long poles.

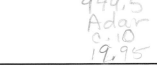

Published by
Crabtree Publishing Company

350 Fifth Avenue   360 York Road, RR 4   73 Lime Walk
Suite 3308   Niagara-on-the-Lake   Headington
New York   Ontario, Canada   Oxford OX3 7AD
N.Y. 10118   L0S 1J0   United Kingdom

Cataloging in Publication Data
Adare, Sierra
    Greece: the land/Sierra Adare.
        p. cm. -- (The lands, peoples, and cultures series)
Includes index.
Summary: Introduces the land of Greece, including the country's
geography, history, industry, agriculture, and wildlife.
ISBN 0-86505-226-3 (rlb). -- ISBN 0-86505-306-5 (pb)
        1. Greece--Description and travel--Juvenile literature.
2. Greece--History--Juvenile literature. [1. Greece.] I. Title.
II. Series: Kalman. Bobbie. 1947- Lands, peoples, and cultures series.
DF728. A33 1999
949.507'6--dc21   LC 98-4497
                                       CIP

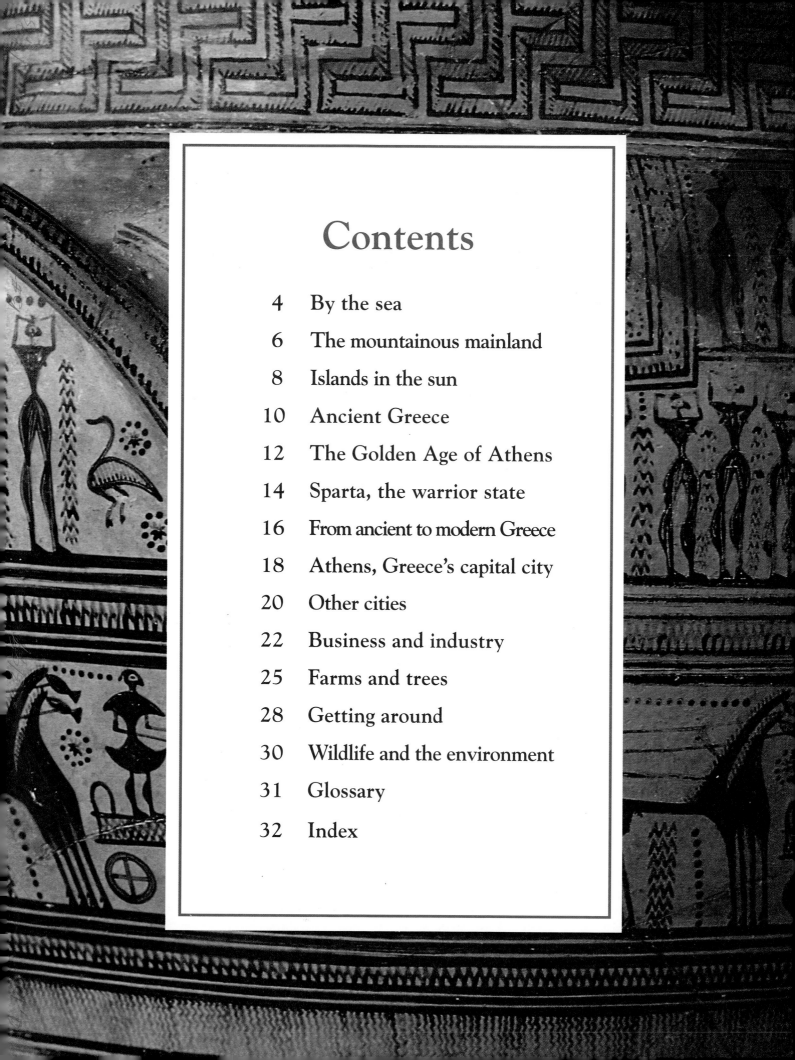

Contents

Homes are built into the rugged coast of Santorini, an island that is the top of a volcano sticking out of the sea.

Few nations have contributed as much to world culture as Greece. Many of our ideas about government, medicine, **architecture**, sports, literature, art, mathematics, law, and **astronomy** have roots that go back to the ancient Greeks. Most of the subjects we study in school were first taught by the Greeks thousands of years ago!

The Greece of today is different from ancient Greece. After centuries of being controlled by other nations, Greece has been an **independent** country since 1830. This makes modern Greece a somewhat young nation. Despite differences between ancient and modern Greece, much of the land has remained as it was centuries ago.

The lure of the sea

For thousands of years, the sea has played an important role in the lives of the Greek people. Even today, many Greeks earn their living from the sea, some by fishing and others by shipping materials from all over the world. The sea also attracts tourists who visit Greece's beautiful beaches, bask in its sunny Mediterranean climate, and spend money on food, hotels, travel, and souvenirs.

(above) A monastery built on the top of a rock formation seems to rise out of Greece's mountainous landscape.

*(opposite page) The peninsula of Peloponnese was once connected to the mainland by the **Isthmus** of Corinth. Today, Peloponnese is divided from the mainland by the Corinth Canal, completed in 1893.*

Wherever you travel in mainland Greece, mountains are not far away. Over three-quarters of the land is covered with mountains. The Pindus range runs down the middle of the country, and the Olympus range lies along the east coast. In most places, the soil is thin and rocky, but between the mountains, in central and northern Greece, lie two large, **fertile** plains.

Mountains divide the mainland of Greece into six main regions, called provinces: Thrace, Macedonia, Thessaly, Epirus, Central Greece, and Peloponnese.

Traditional Thrace

Thrace, in northeastern Greece, is a small province that borders Bulgaria and Turkey. Until 1923, Thrace was part of Turkey, and even today it feels and looks more like Turkey than Greece. People in Thrace's villages wear traditional Turkish-style baggy pants, full shirts, and headdresses. Tobacco, the province's largest crop, is grown in the valleys and on the plains.

Macedonia, the largest province

To the west of Thrace lies Macedonia. This province was once a part of the ancient kingdom of Macedonia, and it shares a border with the Republic of Macedonia, an independent country to the north of Greece. The province of Macedonia also borders Albania and Bulgaria. The province's continental climate brings cold winters and warm summers. Cotton and rice are grown in the huge plain that lies in the middle of the province. The rest of the land is mainly mountainous, and the slopes of Mount Vermio are a center for winter sports.

Thessaly, Greece's breadbasket

Thessaly, in central Greece, is surrounded by high mountain peaks. Summers in this province are very hot, and winter is cold and damp. Thessaly is called "the breadbasket of Greece" because food crops, such as sugar beets and grains, are grown on the fertile plain that lies in the center of the province. Thessaly is also famous for its olives.

Epirus, the mountainous region

Epirus, which lies in the northwest corner of Greece, has majestic mountains and deep valleys. The people of Epirus have kept their traditional customs and dress, partly because the Pindus Mountains isolate the province from the rest of Greece. Shepherds still wander through mountain pastures with their flocks of sheep and goats.

Sunny Central Greece

Most of Central Greece is made up of low hills and plains covered with vineyards, olive groves, and orchards. The climate is milder than in the northern provinces. Part of Central Greece, named Attica, is called "the heart of Greece" because it contains Greece's capital city, Athens, and Piraeus, a busy port. To the east, lies the large island of Euboia, which is connected to the mainland by a bridge.

Peloponnese, the giant to the south

Many of Greece's mountain ranges form long strips of land that reach into the sea as **peninsulas**. Greece's most southern province, Peloponnese, is a vast and mountainous peninsula of high peaks and coastal plains.

The region's Mediterranean climate, with hot, dry summers and mild winters, has made this area famous for the citrus fruits and early vegetables it **exports** to the rest of Europe. Grain fields and olive groves dot the landscape. Small villages are found in sheltered bays along the coast. Higher up in the mountains, stone houses sit on narrow ledges of bare, gray rock cliffs.

Earthquake!

Greece sits on the Balkan Peninsula, which occasionally shakes with earthquakes and milder earth tremors. Ancient Greeks believed earthquakes were caused by angry Poseidon, the god of the sea. A well-known earthquake was reported in the ninth century AD. This quake destroyed Corinth and may have killed as many as 45,000 people. More recently, in the 1950s, several quakes caused much damage in Greece and killed many people, especially on the Ionian islands and Aegean islands.

Islands in the sun

The Greek islands are actually mountain ranges that are mostly under the sea, with just their tops above the water's surface. Greece's more than 1400 islands are **submerged** mountains, but fewer than 200 islands have people living on them. The islands make up one-fifth (20 percent) of Greece's total land area. The largest Greek island is Crete. The other islands are divided into five groups: the Sporades, Ionian, Cyclades, Dodecanese, and Northeastern Aegean islands.

The Sporades

The Sporades islands, which run east of the coast of Thessaly, are known for their fresh seafood, bright sunshine, lush forests, jagged coastlines, and pleasant temperatures. These islands are actually extensions of Mount Pelion, on a peninsula in Thessaly.

The Ionians

The Ionian islands form a chain from Peloponnese up along the western coast of Greece. Corfu, the most northern and best known of these islands, lies about two miles (three kilometers) off the coast of Albania. Tourists flock to Corfu because the temperature is neither too warm nor too cool throughout the year.

The Cyclades

Spread out southeast of Athens in the central and southern Aegean Sea, the Cyclades were named by ancient Greeks for the circular, or cyclical, pattern that they form around the holy island of Delos. The tiniest island of the group, Delos was,

(above) In addition to their golden beaches and rocky terrain, the islands of the Cyclades are known for their blue skies, white houses, and windmills.

according to the ancient Greeks, the birthplace of the god Apollo and his twin sister, Artemis. Today, Delos is one large **archeological** site, and most of its **inhabitants** are people who work at the island's museum and ancient ruins.

The Dodecanese

East of the Cyclades are the Dodecanese, which means "twelve islands" in Greek. The Dodecanese actually have more than twelve islands if you count several smaller ones. The Dodecanese are closer to southwestern Turkey than to the mainland of Greece. Like the Cyclades, they have hot summers and mild winters. Rhodes, the largest and most famous island in the chain, is called the island of the sun. Most Greeks on these islands earn their living from the sea and tourism.

The Northeast Aegeans

The Northeast Aegean islands are scattered throughout the Aegean Sea. Fishing villages along the coasts give way to inland vineyards, olive groves, and pine forests. While tourism has changed many islanders' way of life, wine production, olive growing, and lumbering are still important ways of earning a living. Islanders also make chewing gum from the sticky **resin** that people have been scraping off **mastic** trees since the 1400s.

Crete

Crete's snow-capped mountains rise with breathtaking beauty above its plains and coast. A deep gorge, the largest in Europe, splits Crete's western plain. The largest of the Greek islands, Crete is the site of Europe's oldest civilization, the Minoan, which dates back five thousand years and flourished from 1700 BC to 1400 BC.

Today, Crete has mountain villages, farmland, and modern cities. Many people consider its climate the mildest and healthiest in all of Europe. Winds from the north blow hot and dry during the summer, especially in the interior of the island, where the cool sea breezes are not felt. During the winter, the winds bring rain and cooler temperatures.

Some residents worry that Crete's booming tourist business may make the island too crowded, especially cities such as Herakleion along its northern coast.

Ancient Greece

Archeologists have discovered that during prehistoric times, before written history, wandering tribes of people, called nomads, roamed through what is today Greece. Many centuries later, these wandering people settled into communities. Some of them grew into large and powerful empires.

The Minoan civilization

The area's first great kingdom developed on the island of Crete. King Minos of Crete ruled a civilization that was highly skilled in the arts and the sciences. His subjects and their **descendants** are called Minoans. They built the palace of Knossos around 1700 BC. It was no ordinary palace. It contained more than a thousand rooms surrounding a courtyard. The queen enjoyed such luxuries as a flush toilet and a bath with running water!

The Mycenaeans

Mycenae, the richest and most powerful state in the Mediterranean world at the time, dominated Greece from about 1600 to 1200 BC. It was named after its fortress city, Mycenae, in the Peloponnese. The Mycenaean civilization, with its warrior kings, was destroyed by the Dorians, Greek-speaking invaders from the north.

The rise of the city-states

Towns in ancient Greece were separated by mountains. This isolation led to the growth of the city-state, or *polis*, around 800 BC. Independent city-states grew up around an *acropolis,* the highest point in the area, such as a hill or plateau. A citadel, or fortress, to defend the city against attack, was built on top of the acropolis. A community of houses and farms developed around the citadel. The *agora*, or marketplace, in the center of town, was surrounded by public buildings, such as the

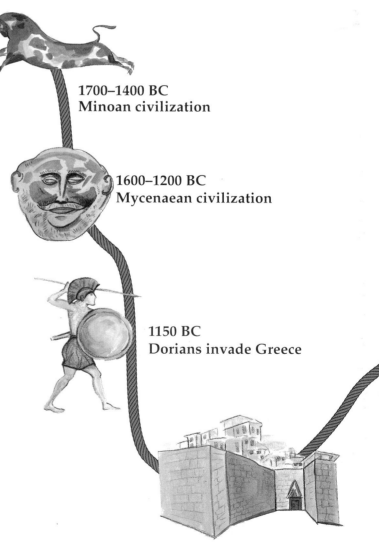

1700–1400 BC
Minoan civilization

1600–1200 BC
Mycenaean civilization

1150 BC
Dorians invade Greece

800 BC
Rise of the Greek city-states

bouleuterion, or council hall, a sports stadium, and temples dedicated to Greek gods and goddesses.

Each city-state had its own ruler and government, its own religious traditions, legends, and sporting events. Each town created its own crafts and grew its own crops, which it traded with other city-states. Two of the most powerful city-states were Athens and Sparta.

(opposite page) A painting of women in blue on the wall of the palace of Knossos, a magnificent structure built on Crete by the ancient Minoans.

The battle of Marathon

In 490 BC, Persia, a mighty empire in the east, decided to attack the city-state of Athens. A huge fleet of Persian ships crossed the Aegean Sea, and twenty thousand archers and cavalry landed near Athens on the Plain of Marathon. The much smaller Athenian army was waiting for them. For eight days a fierce battle raged, and finally the Persians were defeated. The Athenian general sent a trusted messenger to run to Athens and bring the good news. The messenger ran 25 miles (40 kilometers) without stopping, announced the victory, and dropped dead from exhaustion. This event inspired the marathon race, which is now part of the modern Olympic Games.

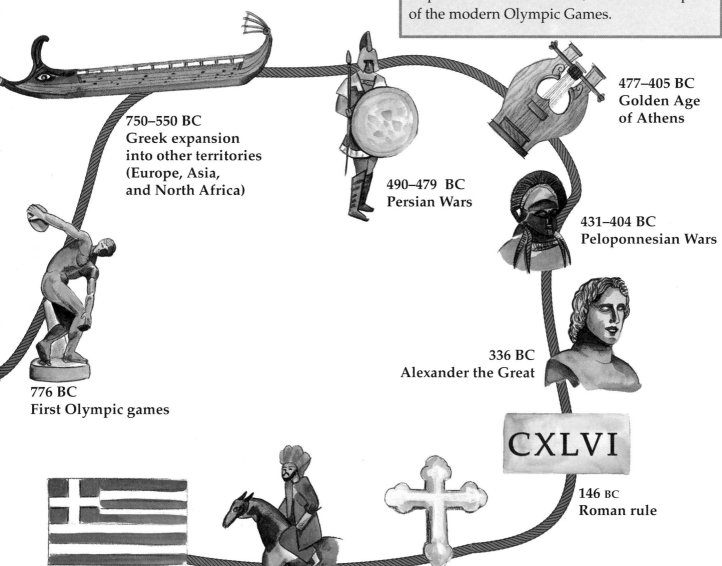

**750–550 BC
Greek expansion
into other territories
(Europe, Asia,
and North Africa)**

**490–479 BC
Persian Wars**

**477–405 BC
Golden Age
of Athens**

**431–404 BC
Peloponnesian Wars**

**776 BC
First Olympic games**

**336 BC
Alexander the Great**

**146 BC
Roman rule**

**1830
Greek independence**

**AD 1453–1829
Turkish Ottoman Empire**

**AD 330–1453
Byzantine Empire**

(opposite page) Modern Athens has spread out around the Acropolis, the center of ancient Athens. (above) Overlooking the city of Athens from the Acropolis is the Parthenon, a temple that still commands the awe of both residents and tourists. Today, Athenians are concerned with preserving the Parthenon and its unique architecture, such as the porch shown here.

Ancient Greece was dominated by two city-states, Athens and Sparta. Although they were very different from each other, both played an important role in the ancient Greek world. After Athens defeated the Persian army, the city enjoyed a period of peace and **prosperity** known as the Golden Age of Athens.

A center for the arts

Athens was named after Athena, the goddess of wisdom, and arts and crafts. The city became a center for arts, science, and literature. It was home to some of the greatest poets, playwrights, **philosophers**, and political leaders in history. Local artisans created fine pottery and jewelry. **Architects** designed magnificent public buildings and temples, filled with bronze, gold, or marble statues of Greek heroes, gods, and goddesses. During the period of peace that followed the war with Persia, Athens built some of its finest buildings, including the Parthenon, a magnificent temple on top of the Acropolis.

Athenian government

Athens was a democracy, which means that the citizens elected their leaders. Every nine days, the *ekklesia*, or elected assembly, met in the agora to pass laws and make decisions. Any citizen, that is any native-born Athenian male who was not a slave, could stand up and speak in the assembly. After all who wished to speak had their say, the discussions ended, and the members of the assembly voted.

Who were the citizens of Athens?

Only free males could choose their leaders and vote. Women, slaves, and former slaves were not considered citizens and could not vote. Slaves who showed exceptional bravery on the battlefield were sometimes given their freedom and Athenian citizenship.

Daily life

Early each morning, the agora, or marketplace, began to fill up with the male citizens of Athens. Businessmen, on their way to work, stopped for a chat. Tradesmen opened their shops or set up stalls selling meat, fish, cheese, and vegetables, wine, pottery, and **textiles**.

Women spent most of their time at home. They lived in a separate section of the house. They planned the meals and wove cloth for the

Slavery

Every Greek city-state had its slaves—men, women, and children captured in war and sold by slave traders in the agora. Slaves cooked, cleaned, and looked after small children. They worked in mines and small factories and on farms. Slaves had no political rights and could not vote.

family's clothes, but often slaves did the cleaning, shopping, and most of the cooking.

After sunset, the men came home for the main meal. Wealthy men often entertained their friends in the evening. They lay on couches, listening to music and poetry, enjoying the food and wine served to them by their slaves.

The other important Greek city-state was Sparta. Spartan citizens were forbidden to work. They depended entirely on *helots*, land slaves who worked on the farms. Because the Spartans were always afraid the helots would revolt, they developed a strong warrior society.

Little culture

Sparta was little more than a collection of wooden houses and farms. It had no magnificent temples, and its people produced few works of art or literature. Today, only a few Spartan ruins remain. They lie outside the modern Greek city of Sparta, in the southeast Peloponnese.

A soldier's life

Every young male citizen of Sparta served as a full-time soldier, called a *hoplite*. He wore a bronze helmet, an armored breastplate, leggings, and a red cloak. He carried a shield, a spear, and sometimes swords or bows and arrows. Hoplites were a fearsome sight as they marched against Sparta's enemies.

Rugged training

In ancient Sparta, children did not belong to their parents but to the state. State officials examined every newborn, and if the baby was sick or weak, it was left to die in the mountains.

At the age of seven, boys were taken from their families to live in military barracks, where they stayed until they were thirty. They were trained for war and taught the values of discipline and a rugged life. They received only one tunic to wear for the entire year. Young boys were whipped to teach them to accept pain. Some let themselves be whipped to death to show their bravery. If a young soldier broke any rules, he lost his

Spartan: You can look it up!

Sparta was a warrior society that produced the best soldiers in ancient Greece. The ancient city-state has left one important reminder of its past: the word *spartan*, which describes someone who shows discipline and courage. It also describes something that is simple, rugged, or without decoration, such as *a spartan lifestyle, a spartan room*, or *a spartan diet*.

(above) This carving of a Spartan warrior was made around 490 BC.

citizenship and the right to own slaves. He was forced to wear special clothing that identified his crime.

Girls and women

Spartan girls had more freedom than other girls in ancient Greece. They exercised and wore short tunics that allowed them to run freely. The state wanted girls to be strong so they would grow up to become mothers of warriors. Like women in other city-states, Spartan women could not vote or hold positions of power.

Sparta's government

Sparta valued security more than personal freedom. It did not have a democratic government and was ruled by kings. Anyone who broke the law or spoke out against the government or its rules could be put to death.

The ups and downs of Sparta's power

Sparta was at the height of its power between the eighth and fourth centuries BC. In 431 BC, Sparta, wanting to end the growing influence of its rival city-state, went to war with Athens. This conflict led to a series of land and sea battles, known as the Peloponnesian Wars. In 404 BC, Sparta defeated Athens. Years of war had weakened all the Greek city-states, however, and they became easy targets for invaders from the north—the Macedonians.

(below) Thousands of years after reaching the height of its power as a mighty city-state, Sparta today is a quiet town in southern Greece.

(above) Alexander the Great fought the Persians at the battle of Issus. He spread Greek ideas and culture throughout his vast empire.

In 338 BC, a Macedonian king, Philip II, invaded Greece, bringing many of the city-states under his control. In 336 BC, Philip was **assassinated**. His twenty-year-old son Alexander became king of Macedonia and ruler of Greece.

Alexander the Great

Alexander was a military genius who never lost a battle. In the three years after he became king, Alexander conquered the rest of Greece. With a combined Greek and Macedonian army, he defeated the mighty Persian empire. Leading his troops east, Alexander conquered every army he met along the way, until he reached the border of India. His soldiers refused to go further, so Alexander turned around and led his tired army home. Alexander died of fever at the age of thirty-two, but during his short life, he had created the largest empire in the world.

The Romans

After Alexander died, his generals fought each other and divided his lands. The empire was never so powerful as it had been under Alexander. It was conquered by the Romans, a mighty civilization to the west. In 146 BC, Greece became a Roman province. Like Alexander, the Romans admired all things Greek and spread Greek culture to other parts of the world.

In Athens, a guard watches over a memorial to those who lost their lives fighting for modern Greece.

The Byzantine Empire

In AD 330, the Roman emperor Constantine moved the capital of the empire from Rome to the ancient Greek city of Byzantium, in what is today Turkey. He renamed the city Constantinople. After Constantine's death, the Roman empire was divided, and Constantinople remained the capital of the eastern part. For one thousand years, this Byzantine empire remained Greek-speaking. In 1453, the Ottomans, or Turks, captured Constantinople and took control of all the empire, including Greece.

Independence

Greece remained a part of the Turkish empire for nearly 400 years, but Greeks dreamed of ruling their own country. In 1821, they revolted against the Turks in a war of independence. In 1830, Greece became an independent country. Today, Greece is a democratic **republic**, with a premier and an elected parliament.

(top) Athens is built around several hills that offer green spaces and a chance to escape the crowded city.

(bottom left) Athenians enjoy the quiet of a street closed to traffic.

(bottom right) A shop sells natural sponges collected by divers from the bottom of the Aegean Sea.

In the 1830s, following independence from Turkish rule, Athens was still a small village of about 4000 people. Gathered beneath the Acropolis were a jumble of small wooden huts, crumbling ruins, and a maze of dirt alleys. Since then, Athens has grown tremendously. Today, four million people, more than one-third of Greece's total population, live in the greater Athens area. Visitors are often surprised to find a huge, sprawling, modern city filled with noise, constant traffic, and crowds of people.

Reminders of the past

Tourists who come to Athens looking for Greece's ancient past will not be disappointed. High atop the Acropolis sits the Parthenon, the magnificent temple built in the fifth century BC. Around the city and its suburbs are many other reminders of the city's ancient Greek, Roman, and Turkish past.

The "urban monster"

Seeking a better life, people pour into the "**urban monster,**" as Athens has been called, from **rural** areas. City housing, roads, and **utilities** have been unable to keep up with the population growth. Possibly most serious of all Athens' big-city problems is air pollution, the result of too many cars. To reduce traffic, Athens is constantly extending its underground rail system and has created areas where no cars are allowed.

In every way, a modern city

Athens is like other modern Western cities, but with a style of its own. Fast-food and pizza restaurants share business with the **tavernas,** the traditional places where Greeks gather to talk, eat, drink, and enjoy music.

Athens is a city that never sleeps. Day and night the streets are filled with traffic. People are still chatting on street corners or walking home from cafés just before dawn. Despite the **congestion** and the poverty in some of its districts, the crime rate is very low, making Athens safe at any hour of the day or night.

A tourist's delight: Pláka

Pláka, one of the most famous districts in Athens, lies at the base of the Acropolis. Built over the ancient city of Athens, Pláka offers Greek and Roman ruins, centuries-old churches, and Turkish **mosques**. Athenians and visitors are drawn to its jumble of steep, narrow streets, restaurants, and shops. Most of the streets are closed to traffic, but at night the sound of music from the cafés and restaurants makes Pláka anything but quiet.

Pláka is also the home of a huge bazaar, the Monastiráki Market, which was the center of the Turkish town when the Turks occupied Greece. Today, it is filled with shops and stalls selling everything from furs, food, and furniture to tourist souvenirs, jewelry, and CDs.

Other cities

Thessalonika

The port of Thessalonika, Greece's second largest city, was founded in 315 BC by a Macedonian general who named it after his wife, the sister of Alexander the Great. Today, Roman ruins, Byzantine churches, and Turkish buildings stand out among the city's modern high-rises. Although it is no longer white, the White Tower is one of the city's most famous landmarks. Built over five hundred years ago, it was used as a prison by the Turks.

Pátras, the great seaport

A major port in the Pelopennese and Greece's third largest city, Pátras is a transportation hub. Many people arrive in Pátras only to make travel connections and leave for somewhere else. The city is an important industrial center and university town. It has a lively carnival season and a summer festival season and many places to eat and socialize. One tourist guide claims that Pátras has the second largest number of bars in all of Europe!

Ioánnina, Ali Pasha's fortress

Ioánnina, which stands on the edge of a large lake in a wide, green valley, is known as the city of Ali Pasha. In 1788, Ali was appointed pasha, or ruler, of the region by the Turks. When he became too powerful, they sent an army of fifty thousand soldiers to surround the city. Ali offered to sign a deal with the Turks, but when he arrived at the meeting place, he found a firing squad waiting for him. Today, Ioánnina is a modern commercial

(above) Thessalonika looks like many Mediterranean seaside cities, with a solid front of apartment blocks rising up the hillside from the shore.

and university city. It has several old mosques dating from Turkish rule.

Rhodes: an ancient capital

The city of Rhodes, for over two thousand years the capital of the island of Rhodes, is a popular tourist resort. It is situated on the northeastern corner of the island of Rhodes, facing the coast of Turkey. The city is divided into two sections: the Old Town and the New Town. Old Town, surrounded by fortress walls built six hundred years ago, is a maze of narrow cobblestone lanes that lead to many reminders of the city's past. New Town is a modern district with hotels, fast-food restaurants, and nightclubs, including an Elvis tribute bar, called Presley's. One local newspaper proudly claims that Rhodes has more discos for every person living there than London, Paris, New York, or Berlin!

Inside the walls of Old Town are many reminders of Rhodes's past: ancient Greek ruins, Byzantine churches, Turkish mosques, and a restored Jewish synagogue. People can go for a steam at some of the city's magnificent Turkish baths. Built in the fifteenth century, they still work!

The Colossus of Rhodes

According to tradition, the Colossus was a huge bronze statue of the sun god Helios, 98 feet (30 meters) high. It is usually shown standing over the harbor of Rhodes, with a foot on each shore and ships passing between its legs. Most historians feel that it probably stood beside the harbor, not above it, however. The Colossus, one of the Seven Wonders of the Ancient World, was toppled by an earthquake in 225 BC. Small copies of the Colussus are sold in souvenir shops all over the island.

Business and industry

Greeks like to run their own businesses. Most of the non-farming work force is employed by small, family-owned businesses often based on the tourist trade, such as shops and cafés. The rest of the labor force works in industries, such as shipping, mining, manufacturing, and food processing.

Tourism: a big business in Greece

One of the largest sources of income in Greece today is tourism. Tourists from all over the world travel to Greece to see its ancient buildings and archeological sites. In the summer, they flock to Greece's beaches and seaside resorts. A new trend, ecotourism, gives tourists activities that

have a low impact on the natural environment. It provides undeveloped areas to hike and bike in national forests and parks, and unspoiled beaches for swimming and sunbathing. Some people, however, would like to see more mountain forests cleared for ski resorts and hotels.

Shipping and shipbuilding

Since ancient times, Greeks have built and sailed ships. Today, Greece is known for its fleet of merchant ships, the third largest in the world. Large freighters carry goods from country to country. The Greeks also own many shipyards, where ships are repaired and new ones are built.

Mining natural resources

Greece mines several natural resources. Most of them are exported to other nations for processing. Bauxite and lignite are two of Greece's most important mineral resources. Bauxite, a claylike material, is the main ore in aluminum. Lignite is a brownish-black soft coal that has a slightly woody texture. Greece also produces magnesium, a silver-white metallic element that burns with a brilliant white flame. It is used for the flash in cameras and to set off fireworks and bombs. For centuries, Greece has been known for its marble, a limestone that can be polished and used in buildings and statues.

From farm to factory

Most manufacturing in Greece is based on the use of farm products, such as cotton (for textiles), tobacco (for cigarettes), fruit (for canning), and grapes (for wine making). Other types of industrial production have grown in recent years. Factories manufacture metal products, rubber, plastics, and electrical machinery. Most of the larger factories are near the nation's two biggest cities, Athens and Thessalonika.

(above) This beach, nestled among the hills on one of the Sporades islands, is a popular tourist spot.

(opposite page) Agios Nikolaos is one of many resort towns on Crete.

(below) Far off the coast of southern Greece, Crete is ideally suited to the shipping business.

A smaller catch

Many foreigners think of fishing as *the* Greek occupation. After all, Greece has a strong **maritime** tradition, a thriving shipbuilding industry, a long and winding coastline, and over 1400 islands.

While fishing is an important economic activity, pollution and the overfishing of coastal waters have hurt the fishing industry. As a result, fishermen have begun fishing in the high seas of the Mediterranean. During the past ten years, Greece has also developed an **aquaculture** industry. Many types of fish are bred and raised on fish farms, much as land farms raise livestock for meat.

(left) A woman sells sponges in the Old Town section of Rhodes. Sponges live in colonies just off the coasts of the Greek islands. Sponge fishing created a huge export for Greece until the manufacture of artificial sponges.

Fishermen tend to their boats and nets in a harbor on Thassos, an island in the northern Aegean Sea.

Farms and trees

Greece is so mountainous, and the soil is so rocky and shallow, that only one-third of the land is farmed. Many of these **cultivated** areas have little rainfall, and the soil is thin and badly eroded. One-quarter of Greece's population still owns or works on farms. Few large forests are left in Greece today, and forestry plays a small role in the country's economy.

A patchwork of tiny farms

Imagine living on a farm that has been passed down from parents to children for many generations. What started out as a large piece of land is divided equally among all the children, who in turn divide their land equally among their children, and so on. The farm has become little plots of land. This is what has happened to many farms in Greece. Often they are so small that they do not make very much money. Many younger people are leaving the farm for jobs in the cities. This **exodus** to the cities creates a shortage of workers during the harvest, but it leaves more land for those who stay behind.

Viniculture: good things from grapes

Viniculture, the tradition of growing grapes for wine, dates back to 3000 BC. Until recently, Greek wines were sold only in Greece. Today, some are being bottled for export to other parts of the world, where they are known for their flavor and quality. The resin, or *retsina,* that Greeks often add to wine gives it a unique taste. Many grapes are also dried into raisins.

(above) Much of Greece is covered with meadows and scrubby woodlands that are so rocky they cannot be farmed.

Grapes, which can be grown on steep hillsides, grow sweet in the hot Greek sun.

Olives: an ancient fruit

Olives and olive oil have been an important part of the Greek diet since ancient times. Olive trees are so abundant in southern and central Greece that growers cannot find enough workers to harvest the groves. Many German and English students are hired at harvest time. They beat the trees to bring down the olives, which are pressed to extract the oil.

Cotton, tobacco, and other crops

Cotton is an important crop for export. It is also the basis of Greece's textile industry. More than half of Greece's cotton crop grows in Thessaly, which is also known for its olives.

The Yellow Plain on the Greek mainland provides perfect conditions for vast fields of tobacco. The sale of tobacco to other countries is important for the Greek economy. Citrus fruits are also exported to European countries where it is too cold for oranges and lemons to grow. Other

Some of the world's finest olive oil is made from Greek olives.

important crops include grains, such as wheat and barley. Rice is grown in some of Greece's river **deltas**.

A man herds his goats on the island of Crete. Goats are numerous in the rocky pastures and hilly regions of Greece.

Livestock

Flocks of sheep and goats are a common sight in Greece. They graze in the rocky pastures on both the mainland and the islands. These animals are raised for their milk and meat. Many Greek dishes use lamb, goat, and *feta*, a tasty goat milk cheese. Cattle, poultry, pigs, and rabbits are also raised.

Forest lands

Compared to agriculture and manufacturing, the forest industry plays a minor role in Greece's economy. Only 19 percent of Greece is covered with forests. Most of the evergreen forests that once covered much of the land have been destroyed in southern Greece. Because they are difficult to reach, the high mountains of northern Greece are still covered with forests. Trees are being planted in **deforested** areas to stop soil **erosion** and to provide much-needed lumber for the building business.

Where have all the forests gone?

About 8000 years ago, much of Greece was covered with thick forests. As more people moved into the region, the forests began to disappear. Over centuries, trees were cut down for shipbuilding and farmland, and grazing goats destroyed new growth in the forests. By the fourth century BC, the Greek philosopher Plato was worried about the cutting down of trees on the hills surrounding Athens.

Today, Greece's forests are still threatened by human development. Each summer, fires destroy large portions of Greek forests and add to the country's air pollution problem. Many of these fires are started by developers, clearing land for construction. Deliberately set fires on the island of Sámos, in the northeast Aegean, have wiped out a third of the pine forests and centuries-old olive groves.

Getting around

As long as they are not trying to get to or from work, most Greeks have a relaxed attitude toward travel around the mainland and the islands. Large families and groups of friends may travel together, and the trip often turns into a social event with music, food, and fun! Sooner or later, they will get to where they are going, but getting there is half the fun.

Island hopping

An extensive ferry service of large, modern ships carries people who have patience and time on their hands to most of the islands. Ferries run frequently among the larger islands during the summer. Because schedules may change at the last moment and some of the smaller islands can be reached only a few times a week, travelers may miss the boat to the island they want to visit. Bad weather may also keep people stranded while they wait for the wind to calm down.

Some people prefer traveling by hydrofoil, a craft that skims across water. Called *Flying Dolphins*, hydrofoils go twice as fast as ferries but cost more. Service can be uncertain because they do not operate in rough seas. Even on a calm day, passengers should expect a bumpy ride!

By car

Greek drivers tend to view traffic signs and signals as things to consider but not necessarily obey. This fact helps explain why Greece competes with Portugal as the country with the highest accident rate in all of Europe. Drivers going uphill almost always claim the right of way, regardless of how an intersection may be marked. Railroad crossings are rarely marked at all.

Greece has only a few expressways. It has many paved highways, but these can unexpectedly turn into dirt roads. In the mountain areas, these roads can be narrow and winding. In the countryside, donkeys and flocks of sheep often compete with cars for room on the road.

By rail

The major Greek railroad, OSE (Hellenic Railways Organization), connects Athens to most major cities. The Greek railway system is neither the fastest nor the most reliable way of getting around the country. Rail lines are limited to the mainland and do not extend to the west coast. Most trains run slowly, and people find buses more convenient for getting from city to city. Athens has a growing subway system, but its expansion is often stalled when workers run across ancient ruins buried beneath the city.

Taxis and buses

Buses are a popular means of travel, and a group of bus companies, known as KTEL, provides inexpensive and dependable service, even to **remote** places. Many KTEL buses are owned by their drivers and are decorated to reflect each owner's tastes. Experienced travelers know to arrive early, because if a bus is making good time on its route, it may leave its stops ahead of schedule.

Those who are adventurous take a taxi. They are fairly inexpensive, but drivers can charge each person individually and often pick up as many people along the way as will fit into the taxi. Riding in a crowded taxi is a chance to meet all sorts of interesting people!

(opposite page) Car ferries, cruise ships, and passenger boats compete with freighters and merchant ships in the harbor at Piraeus, the port city of Athens.

(below) This street scene shows several ways that busy Athenians get around their city. How many methods of transportation can you spot?

Greece has nine national parks, home to wolves, foxes, hares, wild boars, bears, a rare species of white goat found on Crete, and 358 species of birds. Zagorochória, a region in the province of Epirus, provides a haven for rare **chamois**, **lynx**, eagles, and hawks.

Endangered pelicans

The Evros River delta, in Thrace, is a major **sanctuary** for endangered waterfowl. In the north, the Préspa Lakes are nesting grounds for the Dalmatian pelican and the wild pelican, both on the endangered species list. The Greek government has created a national bird sanctuary at these lakes.

Kastoriá: the "beaver place" and the modern fur industry

The Greek fur trade began between five hundred and six hundred years ago and was based on the beavers that lived around Kastoriá Lake. Although the beavers have been hunted out of existence in this area, Kastoriá continues the traditions of the fur industry with hundreds of tailors' and fur cutters' workshops. The furriers of Kastoriá import fur scraps from North America and Scandinavia, sew them into fur coats, and export them to the fashion capitals of Paris, London, and New York.

Urban pollution

Big cities mean cars and factories, and these mean air pollution. In Athens and other cities, people with breathing problems are often told not to go outside in the summer. **Acid rain** and air pollution are destroying Greece's ancient marble monuments. Scientists have developed chemicals that soak into the stone surfaces of statues and temples and glue them together. The mixture does not stick well to marble and must be reapplied every few years. Scientists fear that continuously using chemicals may damage the ancient buildings and do more harm than good.

(top) People and pelicans eye each other.

(bottom) Scientists are trying to rescue ancient buildings and sculptures from the effects of air pollution and acid rain.

Glossary

acid rain Rainfall that has been polluted by fumes from cars and factories

acquaculture raising fish for food

archeologist a person who studies archeology

archeology the study of ancient remains

architect a person who designs buildings

architecture the art of designing buildings

assassinate to murder

astronomy the study of the planets and stars

chamois A small, goatlike animal

congestion Overcrowding

cultivated prepared and used for growing vegetables, fruits, flowers, or other crops

deforested cleared of trees

delta the area between the branches of a river at its mouth

descendants children and grandchildren for many generations

erosion the wearing away

exodus A departure, or leaving, of a large number of people

export To send goods to other countries to be sold or traded

fertile (in land) Able to grow plants and crops independent not controlled by anyone else inhabitant a person who lives in a place

isthmus a narrow piece of land joining two larger pieces of land

lynx A wildcat with a short tail, long legs, and usually tufted ears

maritime connected with the sea

mastic tree A small evergreen shrub that produces a resin used in making chewing gum

mosques a building where Muslims worship

philosopher A person who studies the meaning of life

peninsula A piece of land almost surrounded by water

prosperity a time of having plenty of money

republic a country with an elected government but no king or queen

remote faraway, distant

resin a sticky brown or yellow substance that comes from certain plants

rural belonging to the countryside

sanctuary A natural area where animals and plants are protected

submerged underwater

taverna a Greek restaurant

textile A fabric or type of cloth

Turkish bath A place where people go to take a steam bath

urban belonging to a city

utilities Public services, such as electricity, telephone, water, natural gas, and transportation

Index

acid rain 30

acropolis 10

Acropolis (Athens) 12–13, 19

Aegean Sea 5, 8, 9, 11, 18, 24, 27

agora 10, 12, 13

Albania 5, 6, 8

Alexander the Great 11, 16, 20

ancient Greece 5, 9, 10–11, 12–13, 14–15, 16, 25, 27

aquaculture 24

architecture 5, 12

Athens 5, 7, 11, 12–13, 15, 16, 18–19, 23, 27, 29, 30

Attica 7

Balkan Peninsula 7

Bulgaria 5, 6

buses 29

business and industry 22–23

Byzantine Empire 17, 20, 21

Byzantium 17

Central Greece 5, 6, 7

chewing gum 9

citrus fruits 7, 26

city-states 10–11, 12, 13, 14, 15, 16

Colossus of Rhodes 21

Corfu 5, 8

Corinth 5, 6, 7

cotton 6, 23, 26

Crete 5, 8, 9, 10, 11, 23, 27, 30

Cyclades islands 5, 8–9

Delos 8–9

democracy 12-13, 17

Dodecanese islands 5, 8, 9

Dorians 10

earthquakes 7

ecotourism 22

endangered animals 30

environment 30

Epirus 5, 6, 7, 30

Euboia 5, 7

farming 23, 25–27

ferries 28–29

fishing 5, 9, 24

food crops 7

forests 8, 9, 22, 25, 27

fur industry 30

gods and goddesses, Greek 9, 11, 12

Golden Age of Athens 11, 12–13

hydrofoils 28

Ioánnina 5, 20

Ionian islands 5, 7, 8

islands 8–9, 24, 28

Jews 21

Kastoria 30

Knossos, palace of 10, 11

Macedonia 5, 6

Macedonians, ancient 15, 16, 20

Marathon 5, 11

Mediterranean Sea 5, 7, 10, 20, 24

mining 22, 23

Minoan civilization 9, 10, 11

Minos, King 10

Mount Olympus 5, 6

Mount Pelion 5, 8

mountains 6–7, 8, 9, 25, 27

Mycenae 5, 10

Mycenaean civilization 10

natural resources 23

Northeastern Aegean islands 5, 8, 9

olives 7, 9, 26, 27

Olympic Games 11

Ottoman Empire 17

Parthenon 12–13, 19

Pátras 5, 20

Peloponnese 5, 6, 7, 10, 14, 20

Peloponnesian Wars 11, 15

peninsula 7

Persia 11, 12, 16

Philip II 16

Pindus Mountains 5, 6, 7

Piraeus 5, 7, 29

Pláka 18–19

pollution 19, 24, 27, 30

population 8, 19, 25

railroads 28, 29

Republic of Macedonia 5, 6

Rhodes 5, 9, 21, 24

rice 6

Romans, ancient 11, 16, 17, 19

ruins, ancient 9, 14, 19, 20, 22, 29, 30

Santorini 4

Seven Wonders of the Ancient World 17

shipbuilding 22, 24, 27

shipping 5, 22, 23

slavery 12, 13, 14, 15

Sparta 5, 11, 12, 14–15

sponges 18, 24

Sporades islands 5, 8, 23

textiles 13, 23, 26

Thessalonika 5 20, 23

Thessaly 5, 6–7, 26

Thrace 5, 6, 30

tobacco 6, 23, 26

tourism 5, 8, 9, 19 20, 21, 22, 23,

transportation 19, 28–29

Turkey 5, 6, 9, 17, 19, 20, 21

vineyards 7, 9

viniculture 23, 25

war of independence 17

wildlife 30

women 13, 15

1 2 3 4 5 6 7 8 9 0 Printed in the USA 5 4 3 2 1 0 9 8